Campbell Kids

Kids

A SOUPER CENTURY

⚜ ⚜ ⚜ ⚜ ⚜

Campbell Kids™

A SOUPER CENTURY

⚜ ⚜ ⚜ ⚜ ⚜ ARIC CHEN ⚜ ⚜ ⚜ ⚜ ⚜

Harry N. Abrams, Inc., Publishers

Editor: Linas Alsenas
Designed by Elizabeth Morrow-McKenzie
Production Manager: Jonathan Lopes

Library of Congress Cataloging-in-Publication Data:
Chen, Aric.
The Campbell Kids : a souper century / Aric Chen.
p. cm.
ISBN 0-8109-5043-X
1. Campbell Kids (Advertising characters) 2. Advertising characters—United States—History—20th century.
3. Campbell Soup Company—History—20th century. 4. Advertising—Soup—United States—History—20th century.
5. Advertising—Social aspects—United States—History—20th century. 6. United States—Social life and customs—History—20th century. I. Title.

HF6146.A27C48 2004
659.19'66465—dc22
2004012587

Harry N. Abrams, Inc.
100 Fifth Avenue
New York, NY 10011
www.abramsbooks.com

Abrams is a subsidiary of LA MARTINIÈRE
GROUPE

A NOTE TO THE READER

This book is an introduction to and celebration of the many uses and appearances of the Campbell Kids over the past century. Every effort has been made to
date the images in this book as accurately as possible by decade. However, much of the artwork in this book was created for advertising purposes, and it was common
to reuse, adapt, and imitate earlier images. Moreover, the cropping of many of the illustrations here was determined by the artwork available, which was often lovingly preserved
in scrapbooks by collectors. Identifying captions have not been applied to the illustrations (which appeared in magazine and newspaper advertisements, internal
company reports, and other publications) and objects (such as dolls, tableware, and various toys) because full background information is not available for every image.

STRT YOUR DAY
WITH MUSIC

AND START YOUR
MEALS WITH SOUP

CONTENTS

1900s

1910s

1920s

1930s

clip-
and
save!

1940s

1950s

1960s

1970s

1980s

1990s

TODAY...

...AND TOMORROW

Campbell Kids

INTRODUCTION

They have no individual names, nor are they of any determinate age. There is no set number of them, nor is their relationship to each other ever explained. How is it, then, that the Campbell Kids are so intimately familiar to generations of Americans?

For one hundred years, these rosy-cheeked, cherub-faced youngsters have grown with the country, reflecting its cultural shifts while espousing its ideals and aspirations. They have promoted the Red Cross, inspired Americans to buy war bonds and, later, encouraged children to conserve electricity and build self-esteem. They've donned costumes of all nations, traveled to locales far and wide, played grown-up and dress-up, and, of course, rollicked in good-natured fun. And all the while, they have heartily and happily slurped their Campbell soup.

For sure, the Campbell Kids are fundamentally advertising devices. Yet advertising and popular culture have long been inseparable twins. The Kids have thrived as emblems of both, and the secrets of their longevity lie in the values and relentless optimism of America itself. With their well-meaning innocence, the Kids have in many ways transcended their original role of personifying youthful vigor, taste, nutrition, and quality to more broadly embody goodness, wholesome living, and wide-eyed curiosity. There is no hint of cynicism, sloth, or mean-spiritedness in their company.

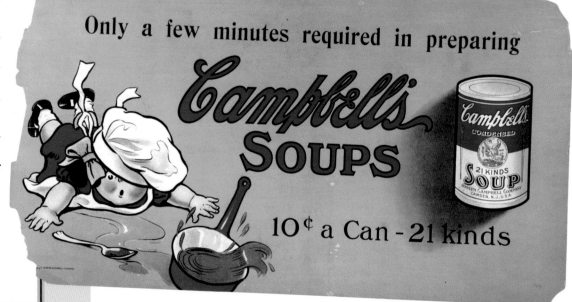

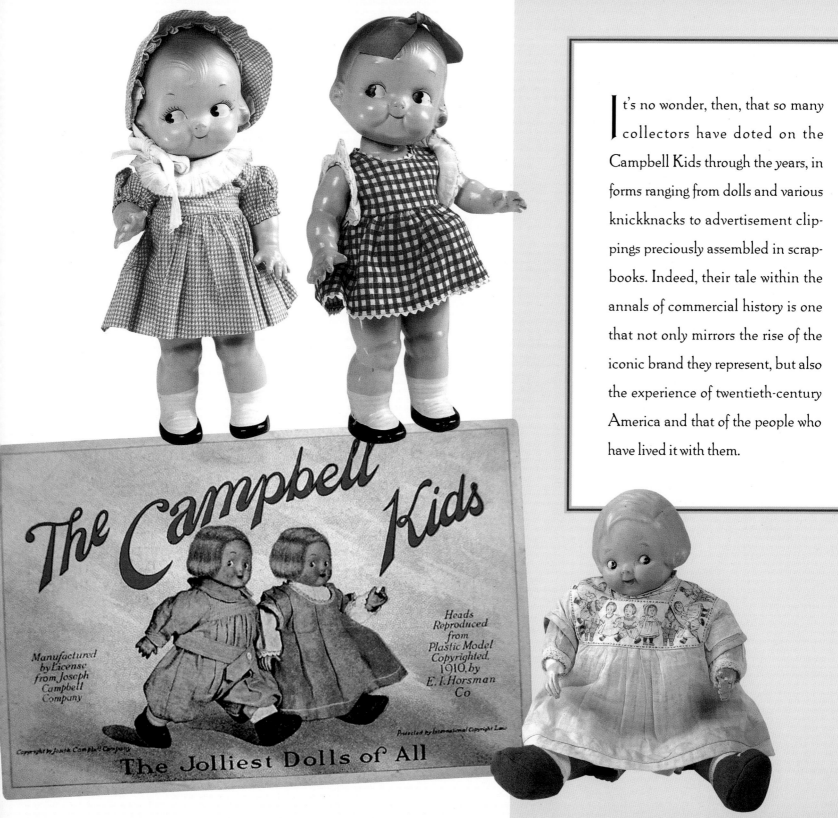

It's no wonder, then, that so many collectors have doted on the Campbell Kids through the years, in forms ranging from dolls and various knickknacks to advertisement clippings preciously assembled in scrapbooks. Indeed, their tale within the annals of commercial history is one that not only mirrors the rise of the iconic brand they represent, but also the experience of twentieth-century America and that of the people who have lived it with them.

The Campbell Kids

Manufactured by License from Joseph Campbell Company

Heads Reproduced from Plastic Model Copyrighted, 1910, by E. I. Horsman Co

Protected by International Copyright Law

Copyright by Joseph Campbell Company

The Jolliest Dolls of All

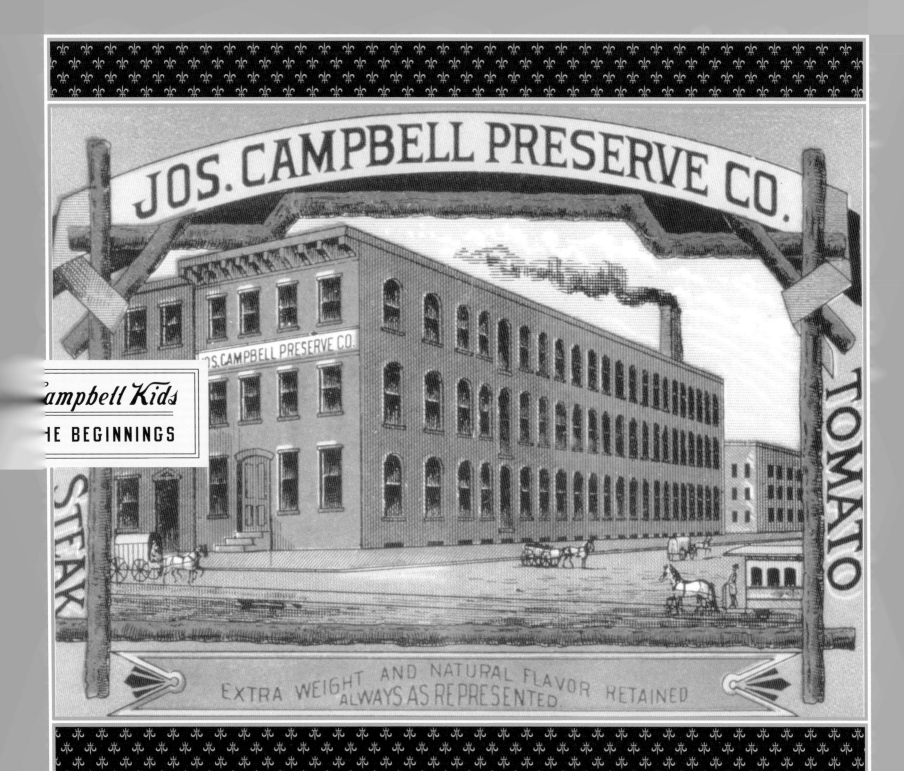

JOS. CAMPBELL PRESERVE CO.

JOS.CAMPBELL PRESERVE CO.

Campbell Kids

THE BEGINNINGS

STEAK

TOMATO

EXTRA WEIGHT AND NATURAL FLAVOR RETAINED
ALWAYS AS REPRESENTED.

THE STORY OF THE CAMPBELL KIDS begins in 1869, thirty-five years before their actual inception. That year, Abraham Anderson and Joseph Campbell opened their Anderson & Campbell cannery across the Delaware River from Philadelphia in what was then the growing manufacturing town of Camden, New Jersey. Rapid industrialization called for less perishable foods that could survive the ever-widening distances separating the field and the urban dinner table, and Anderson and Campbell's partnership was a recipe for success. First, they were conveniently located between the fertile farms of New Jersey and the commercial and transportation hub of Philadelphia. Second, there was the complementary expertise of the men themselves. Anderson was a trained tinsmith who had opened a cannery seven years earlier after stints applying his craft to both roofing and the relatively new invention of the icebox. Campbell was a farm boy turned fruit and vegetable agent. Together, they canned everything from condiments and mincemeats to peas, asparagus, and, especially, the "Celebrated Beefsteak Tomato," touted as being big enough for each fruit to fill an entire can. The company's overall claims were apparently justified, as it won a medal for quality at Philadelphia's 1876 Centennial Exposition.

That same year, however, Anderson and Campbell parted ways—apparently amicably—in disagreement over the company's pace of expansion. Campbell, the more ambitious of the two, bought the other out, and eventually brought new investors into what soon became Joseph Campbell & Company and then, in 1891, the Joseph Campbell Preserve Company. (The Campbell Soup Company name wouldn't appear until 1922.) One of these partners was Arthur Dorrance, a wealthy lumber and flour merchant who, after Campbell retired, assumed control in 1894. It was Dorrance's nephew, Dr. John Thompson Dorrance, who would conceive the product that would catapult the company into fame and prominence.

At just twenty-four, the younger Dorrance joined his uncle's firm in 1897. He had recently returned from Europe, where he had received a doctoral degree in organic chemistry from Germany's University of Göttingen and had also developed a taste for Continental soups. At the time, American firms like Franco-American (which the company would acquire in 1915) and Huckins were making ready-to-eat soups, and Borden had perfected the process for evaporating milk—but no one had brought the two ideas together in the form of condensed soup. It was up to the energetic junior Dorrance to cook up the invention, which, he correctly reasoned, when implemented "would cost less to ship, would take less room in the store, and could be sold for less to the housewife."

WE SELECT
THE VERY BEST OBTAINABLE
FRESH MEATS, BUTTER AND VEGETABLES.
WHICH ARE BLENDED WITH
FRESH HERBS

IN PREPARING
OUR SOUPS
THIS ALONE IS THE
SECRET OF THEIR
HIGH QUALITY.

PRESERVE CO.
U.S.A.

A year later, the Joseph Campbell Preserve Company was selling five varieties of condensed soups. By 1900, the company had earned the gold medallion for excellence from the Paris International Exposition and had adopted the signature red and white colors—suggested by a company executive who admired them on Cornell University's football team uniforms—that remain affixed on its cans today. By 1905, it was advertising "21 Kinds of Campbell's Soup—16 Million Cans Sold in 1904."

Campbell's SOUPS

10c.

Rich, nourishing and substantial. Made from the best that grows in the heart of New Jersey's finest farming district. High grade in every sense of the words. Over

SIXTEEN MILLION

cans sold in 1904. Everything is done. The blend, the pare, the toil, the care. All you need do is:

"Just Add a Can of Hot Water and Serve"

One can makes sufficient Soup for the average family.

21 Kinds

Joseph Campbell Co.
Dept. A
Camden, N. J.

Particular Soups for Particular People

Campbell's SOUPS

One trial convincing
21 kinds - 10¢ a Can

Campbell's CONDENSED 21 KINDS SOUP JOSEPH CAMPBELL COMPANY CAMDEN, N.J. U.S.A.

THE YEAR 1904 ALSO MARKED THE ARRIVAL OF THE CAMPBELL KIDS. BACK then, Teddy Roosevelt was in the White House and the Wright brothers were testing their new flying machine at Kitty Hawk. In advertising, a character named Sunny Jim was extolling the virtues of Force Cereal. The National Biscuit Company had its own champion in Zu Zu the ginger snap clown. And a dog named Nipper listened obediently to a phonograph manufactured by another Camden-based company that would later become part of RCA. Except for the faithful Nipper, the Campbell Kids would outlast these promotional peers as beneficiaries of one of the most active and widespread advertising programs in history. But before they populated newspapers, magazines, and television commercials, the Kids were more simply known for riding trolleys in New York City.

The Joseph Campbell Preserve Company pioneered the use of streetcar advertising in 1899. The company figured its target consumers were women who, it was thought, were more inclined to ride than walk. "Car cards" promoting the company's soups first surfaced that year on one-third of all streetcars in New York City and within three years, their use expanded to 378 cities. Almost invariably, they featured four-line rhyming jingles by Philadelphia ad man Charles Snyder, who soon recommended incorporating a mascot as well. As the story goes, Theodore Wiederseim, Jr., an employee of the Ketterlinus Lithographic Manufacturing Company, got wind of this. He was seeking a share of the company's lucrative car card business, and he asked his wife, Grace, a freelance illustrator of children's books and comic strips, to add some of her round and jolly toddlers to the layouts he was proposing. From this casual request, the Campbell Kids were born.

Born in 1877 as Viola Grace Gebbie, Wiederseim's wife was the daughter of a successful Philadelphia art publisher who so detested her own first name that she dropped it altogether in her youth. She was by all accounts a charming and gregarious woman of a buoyant, cheerful temperament who undoubtedly possessed an independent spirit as well. In 1911 she both divorced Wiederseim and married the socially prominent W. Heyward Drayton, and they, too, would divorce in 1923. However, she would continue to be known as Grace Gebbie Drayton until her death in New York in 1936.

Growing up in her family's Victorian home, ornately decorated with cherub-adorned art and objects, Drayton—who would have no children of her own—was a precocious illustrator. Early on, she showed an affinity for drawing small-fry characters that, it turns out, were modeled after herself. "I was much interested in my looks. I knew I was funny," she recalled in a 1926 newspaper interview. "I used to look in the mirror, and then, with a pencil in my round, chubby fingers, I would sketch my image as I remembered it." Even in adulthood, her full figure, round face, pug nose, and wide-set eyes bore a remarkable resemblance to the children she adoringly created. Such characters, or "roly-polys," as she sometimes called them, made Drayton one of the most successful commercial illustrators of her time, as she chronicled the adventures of Dolly Dingle, Dimples, Kaptin Kiddo, and others in children's books and publications ranging from the *New York Herald* and *Saturday Evening Post* to *St. Nicholas* and *Ladies Home Journal*.

However, her most famous "funny babies," as she also referred to them, would be the Campbell Kids. Representing the era's picture of health and wholesomeness, these pudgy tots became the voice of Snyder's jingles, proclaiming Campbell soups' quality, taste, and nutrition on streetcars beginning in 1905. Also that year, they made an appearance in the company's first magazine advertisement in *Ladies Home Journal* and, four years later, in Campbell's newspaper debut in the *Saturday Evening Post.* Drayton's Kids had romped their way into the public imagination and to instant popularity. So many families requested copies of the streetcar ads that the company—no doubt seeing the value in encouraging their infatuation—found it prudent to only charge fifteen cents to cover postage. The first Campbell Kid doll, a stuffed velvet figure, appeared in 1909, with a more recognizable successor made by the E. I. Horsman company, and advertised with the slogan "Can't Break 'Em Heads," following in 1910. By 1912, Americans were buying thousands of these Campbell Kid dolls through the Sears, Roebuck and Montgomery Ward catalogs. They were also sending Campbell Kid postcards—a million of which were printed by 1912—while they kept score on Campbell Kid bridge tallies, set tables with Campbell Kid place cards, and wore "I am a Campbell Kid" lapel pins. Even the company's own stationery proclaimed "The Home of the Campbell's Kids."

To be the ice-man
Is my lot,
But give me Campbell's
Piping-hot!

The HOME of the
CAMPBELL'S KIDS

Campbell Soup Company
Camden, New Jersey, U. S. A.
October Seventeenth
1929.

My tummy is empty,
Just begging, it seems,
For Campbell's Tomato,
The soup of my dreams!

Miss Nancy Fagarty,
32 E. Mt. Pleasant Ave.,
Mt. Airy, Philadelphia, Pa.

Dear Miss Nancy:-

It was very nice to hear from you again and we are sending you some of the very old Campbell's Kid illustrations which you requested and two full size Campbell's Kid pictures.

The Campbell's Kiddies have been drawn to show the joyous benefits of good health brought about by eating the right foods, getting plenty of sleep and fresh air.

To allow you and your Mother to become better acquainted with the many delicious Soups prepared in the Campbell's Kitchens we are enclosing a detailed description of each.

Let us hear from you again, Nancy, at any time you want more of the latest Campbell's Kids and we will send them.

Yours very truly,

CAMPBELL SOUP COMPANY,

By

Eat Soup and Keep Well!

From
The CAMPBELL'S KIDS
Campbell Soup Company
Camden, New Jersey, U. S. A.

CAMDEN
OCT 17
2   1929
6 PM
N. J.

Miss Nancy Fagarty,
32 E. Mt. Pleasant Ave.,
Mt. Airy, Philadelphia, Pa.

THE OPTIMIST

Campbell's Daily
VICTORY!

CAPTURE OF
GENERAL APPETITE

THE OPTIMIST

NOVEMBER, 1917

THE OPTIMIST

MARCH, 1914

THE OPTIMIST

THE OPTIMIST

THE OPTIMIST

AUGUST, 1916

With no neck or ears, large heads, and H-shaped mouths, the Campbell Kids have until very recently held on to their defining features despite the number of artists and ad agencies that have served as their custodians. Though she was creating new Kids well into the 1920s, Drayton appears to have been their primary artist only until around 1916, when Roy Williams of the *Philadelphia Public Ledger* was given charge. Subsequent artists have included Corinne Pauli, beginning around 1926; Dorothy Jones in the 1940s and 1950s; the Paul Fennell studio in Hollywood, California, which produced many of the Kids' television commercial appearances of the 1950s; New York's Johnstone & Cushing agency; Mel Richman of Philadelphia; and Richard

Edmiston, who applied his hand for twenty years beginning in 1971.

Through the years, as children will do, the Campbell Kids have also changed in their appearance, and they've done so to reflect the fluctuating moods and fascinations of America. Drayton's Kids, for example, projected the relentless faith in progress and can-do spirit of their age. After all, the company's in-house publication was called *The Optimist*. First issued in 1912, each installment featured everything from poetry and tomato crop reports to ruminations on patriotism and loyalty, and the Kids were used on nearly every cover until 1934. Meanwhile, in advertisements, they were seen testing early versions of the automobile, airplane, and telephone, or, during World War I, promoting strength and

Uncle Dan, the grocery man;

MARCH 1929

vitality at home as they soldiered on in uniform. Often they were juxtaposed with more naturalistically rendered family and home scenes. The company also occasionally published menu and recipe books, including the 1916 *Helps for the Hostess* booklet, a treatise on etiquette and good manners on the cover of which a tuxedoed, white-gloved Campbell boy with a cane and stovepipe hat walked hand-in-hand with his counterpart, in her fur-trimmed coat and pearls.

Although the Kids were used in nearly every company advertisement until 1922, they've also had their ups and downs, and from time to time they have been allowed a well-earned rest.

During the latter years of the Great Depression, for example, they were judged ill-suited to the grim economic times. World War II was also hard on the Kids, and it didn't help that newsprint and tin rationing forced cuts in both advertising in general and soup production for the consumer market. Nevertheless, they experienced another heyday in the 1950s, as the rising medium of television lent them a new onscreen role that also took advantage of that decade's growing emphasis on domesticity. They faded once more in the 1960s and 1970s as company advertising focused on real-life eating situations. However, at no point did they disappear completely.

While they occasionally played second string, they were never totally sidelined, and by the 1980s, Campbell Kid nostalgia was riding high. Licensed products, from ties and watches to sleeping bags and backpacks, all sporting vintage Kid images, peaked in a way not seen since the 1950s. (That's when Campbell Kid vacuum cleaners, kitchen sets, and bicycles were featured in multi-page advertisements in *Life* magazine.) At the same time, the Kids adapted to the country's changing demographics while confronting its pressing social concerns. It was in the '80s that they achieved ethnic diversity, slimmed down in response to youth fitness worries, and embarked on public service campaigns that promoted child self-esteem.

As they enter their second century, the Campbell Kids show no signs of slowing down. On skateboards, on rollerblades, and surfing online, they are keeping up

THE CAMPBELL'S KIDS AT THE CIRCUS

"WE ARE THE FAMOUS CAMPBELL'S KIDS
YOU CERTAINLY MUST KNOW, SIR.
WOULD YOU BE KIND AND LET US IN,
WE WANT SO MUCH TO GO, SIR!"

"JUST STEP RIGHT IN - NO MONEY PLEASE!"
THE TICKET-TAKER CRIED,
FOR HE WAS OVERJOYED TO HAVE
SUCH FAMOUS GUESTS INSIDE!

AND NOW BENEATH THE MAMMOTH TENT
THE CAMPBELL'S KIDS APPEAR;
THE CROWD STANDS UP, THE CROWD APPLAUDS
THE MOMENT THEY DRAW NEAR!

UPON THE PRANCING SNOW-WHITE STEED
THEY'RE ASKED TO TAKE A RIDE;
OH, NOW YOU SEE THEM SPARKLE IN
THEIR HEALTH AND JOY AND PRIDE!

WHAT NOW? OH MY! JUST HOLD YOUR BREATH,
THEY'RE ON THE HIGH TRAPEZE!
AND WHAT A THRILL THEY GIVE, MY LADS,
WITH ALL THEIR STRENGTH AND EASE!

OF ALL THE ACTS AND HITS THAT DAY
THESE KIDS WERE PICKED THE WINNER.
THE MANAGER, TO SHOW HIS THANKS,
SERVED CAMPBELL'S SOUP FOR DINNER!

with real kids in the way they live today. Still, we can rest assured that the Kids will be pushed even further. What may become the next crop of Campbell Kids, introduced at the end of this book, is surely proof of that. Future generations will likely learn what generations before have already known: The Campbell Kids are cute, sweet, and versatile. But they have also proven themselves to be timeless..

Campbell Kids
1900s

FROM THE WRIGHT BROTHERS' FLYING MACHINE TO THE WORLD SERIES and the Teddy Bear, the first decade of the twentieth century was a decade of firsts, and the Campbell Kids were in on the action. Indeed, while Dorothy and friends began their trip down the yellow brick road and Henry Ford delivered his first (pre-assembly line) Model T, the Joseph Campbell Preserve Company was on a roll of its own. For one, it had a shiny new gold medallion from the 1900 Paris International Exposition, as well as twenty-one new varieties of soup. Arriving in 1904 in the midst of all-around progress, the Campbell Kids frolicked their way into the hearts and minds of a nation clamoring for some soup-slurping fun. And so, first in New York City streetcar advertisements and then in magazines and newspapers, illustrator Grace Gebbie Drayton's "funny babies" chimed in with jolly jingles that carried the upbeat mood. Playing in the kitchen, getting into mischief, and being just plain sweet, these plump and pudgy toddlers animated everything from postcards and bridge tallies to place cards and lapel pins, with which children across the country declared, "I am a Campbell Kid."

Campbell's Soup,
bell's chest,
pirate chief,
Soups are best.

12¢

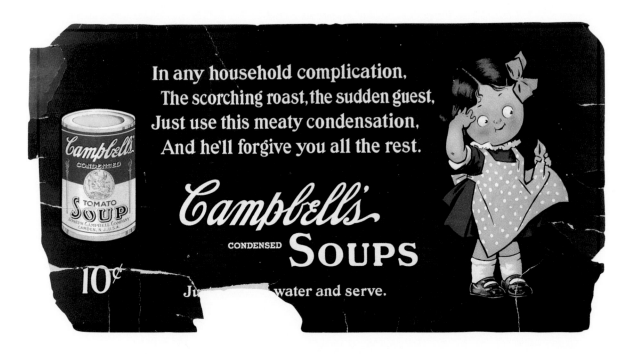

In any household complication,
The scorching roast, the sudden guest,
Just use this meaty condensation,
And he'll forgive you all the rest.

Campbell's CONDENSED SOUPS

10¢

Ju___ ___ water and serve.

"A song of spring is in the air
While youth and joy abound,
And everywhere this *Campbell's* fare
Makes spring the whole year round."

21 Kinds   10¢ a Can

Campbell's SOUPS

*Midnight: hungry,
Sleepless, too;
Here's the quickest
Thing to do—*

For That Hurry Hunger:

When you want a treat that tickles the palate and tones the system;

That gives you something to digest and no trouble to digest it;

That is the best you can get, no matter what else you have in the refrigerator;

That has savor, body, tone—then:

Campbell's SOUPS

10¢

Moreover, one 10-cent can makes sufficient for the average family.

They are prepared by people trained through many years for that purpose.

You, yourself, could not make them better, no matter how cleanly, how skillful, or how careful you are.

And, last but not least, all you need do is

"Just add hot water and serve"

¶ Send for booklet No. 89. It will tell you why the Campbell method of soup making is superior from every standpoint. The illustrations, beautifully lithographed in colors, will entertain the children and interest their elders. Address:

Joseph Campbell Company
26-46 River Street
Camden, New Jersey, U. S. A.

When writing to advertisers please mention Ainslee's

Joseph Campbell Company
31-51 Front Street
Camden, N. J.

Twinkle, twinkle little
star,
I've discovered what you
are,
Just a message from the
blue,
To send up a can or two.

Come an' be a
Campbell Kid;
Best in all creation:
All you need's
an appetite,
For the 'nitiation.

A stitch in
time;
Time for the
stitch —
And then enjoy
This comfort
rich.

Little Jack Horner
sat in a corner,
Having the grand-
est time
With the finest treat
that a boy could
eat,
And it only
cost a
dime.

JOSEPH CAMPBELL COMPANY
31-51 Front Street
Camden, N. J.
U.S.A.

Send for handsome
illustrated booklet
No. 31.

Ready in a wink
For the sudden
guest.
No heat, no hurry;
No waste, no worry.

AMERICA WAS RISING AS A WORLD POWER, AND THE CAMPBELL KIDS WERE enjoying a rise of their own. By the end of the 1910s, they'd made their way into every Campbell advertisement as they busily found new ways to keep up with the times. Etiquette and good manners were the rules of the day, and the Kids gave handy hints to housewives in company-published booklets like *Helps for the Hostess*. However, Campbell girls also knew their entitlements and, at the height of the Progressive Era, marched alongside the suffrage movement and demanded the right to vote. Meanwhile, a Campbell boy put on a Charlie Chaplin moustache and bowler hat and discovered the silver screen, while Campbell Kid dolls were featured in the catalogs of Sears, Roebuck and Montgomery Ward. There they were ordered up by the hundreds of thousands. The decade would also see darker moments as World War I raised the specter of a War to End All Wars. But the Kids rose to the challenge, selling Liberty Bonds and reminding their compatriots that "As President Wilson says, economy does not mean denying yourself plenty of wholesome food."

HELPS FOR THE HOSTESS

COMPLIMENTS
OF THE
MAKERS OF
Campbell's
SOUPS

"Votes for women, yes, you bet
That good time will reach us yet.
When men folks know how house-
work feels
We'll have Campbell's Soup at all
our meals."

10¢ a can

Campbell's SOUPS 10¢ a Can

GIVE VIGOR AND STRENGTH

SCHOOL

CAMPBELL'S KIDS

Nº 2

Campbell Kids
1920s

IT WAS THE JAZZ AGE AND PROHIBITION ERA AND A TIME OF GREAT prosperity. The roaring '20s were high-flying years and the Kids took part in the jubilation. Campbell girls feverishly threw on their flapper dresses to jig and dance the Charleston. Meanwhile, other Kids chatted away on the increasingly ubiquitous telephone just as a growing fascination with flight, propelled by Lindbergh's famous transatlantic journey, sent them airborne in planes of their own. The rise of the skyscraper also lifted them skyward as they rode construction cranes to ever more dizzying heights, while the discovery of King Tut's tomb unleashed a worldwide Egyptian craze that swept them away to the Nile. However, by now it was time to slow things down. Though they continued to make frequent appearances, the Kids were no longer included in every company advertisement, which was just as well, as the stock market crash of 1929 foreshadowed troubling days ahead.

Hip, hip, hurray for Christmas Day,
My train spins round the loop
I'm feeling gay most every way
And full of Campbell's Soup!

SERVE
SOUP
EVERY DAY

CORN LEEKS TOMATOES

CELERY CARROTS

BABY LIMAS ALPHABET MACARONI

PARSLEY SWEET POTATOES ONIONS

PEAS WHITE POTATOES TURNIPS

BARLEY CABBAGE BEEF BROTH

OKRA 15 OTHER INGREDIENTS

Campbell Kids
1930s

THE LEAN YEARS OF THE GREAT DEPRESSION WERE ALSO SLUGGISH
Times for the Campbell Kids. But these indefatigable youngsters still put on a good face. They cheered a dispir-
ited public with their encouraging jingles and introduced the new "M'm! M'm! Good!" slogan that they'd chant for
decades to come. As Americans increasingly looked for distraction in radio,
as well as a Hollywood in its golden age, Campbell Kid voices
briefly hit the airwaves in company advertisements on
shows like *Amos 'N Andy.* But without their irresistible
countenances, their broadcast career was both limited
and short-lived. However, as policemen and utility
workers, and circus trainers and drummer boys, they
secured other roles in service and entertainment,
providing just a little reassurance in a time of great need.

COME AND GET IT!

DICK POWELL
STARRING IN
"HOLLYWOOD HOTEL"
Fridays
9-10 P.M. (E.D.S.T.)
COLUMBIA NETWORK
Coast-to-Coast

A flower for
The clever winner--
And Campbell's Soup
To start her dinner!

With Campbell's for
Your appetite,
You won't go searching
Food tonight!

"Guess what I want for lunch!"

Her eagerness for Campbell's Vegetable Soup shows what a healthy, wholesome, normal appetite she has. Boys and girls are naturally fond of this famous soup because it tastes so mighty good and because it is real, substantial food—just the kind that quiets the steady, gnawing hunger of the active child.

Every spoonful is laden with the finest garden vegetables cooked in rich beef broth to save their healthful goodness in full strength. It's all in the soup—to delight your children's taste and benefit them regularly and often. And it's made in the world's greatest soup-kitchens—universally trusted for strict purity and quality.

LOOK FOR THE
RED-AND-WHITE LABEL

EAT SOUP
AND KEEP WELL

Mother's willing
Helpers we—
Campbell's Soups
And busy Me!

21 kinds to choose from ..

Asparagus	Mulligatawny
Bean	Mutton
Beef	Ox Tail
Bouillon	Pea
Celery	Pepper Pot
Chicken	Printanier
Chicken-Gumbo	Tomato
Clam Chowder	Tomato-Okra
Consommé	Vegetable
Julienne	Vegetable-Beef
Mock Turtle	Vermicelli-Tomato

10 cents a can

Campbell's Vegetable Soup

A real boy's soup!

Active, growing boys—and their sisters, too —are hungry so much of the time that any mother is grateful for a soup which is extra nourishing and substantial. Children are naturally fond of delicious soup because of its tempting flavor. It's an ideal way to delight the ravenous appetite of the normal child.

Campbell's Vegetable Soup! See how the youngsters go for it every time you serve it! Notice how eagerly they eat it. *And* watch their hunger subsiding as they enjoy this hearty soup, this "meal-in-itself!"

Teeming with health-giving vegetables, too— don't forget that. And in a form that children really like. The fine garden vegetables are cooked in rich beef broth which retains their goodness in full strength in this beneficial soup. Serve it regularly and often!

EAT SOUP
AND KEEP WELL

Campbell's Soup
Is what you need
To give you all
My pep and speed!

21 kinds to choose from...

Asparagus	Mulligatawny
Bean	Mutton
Beef	Ox Tail
Bouillon	Pea
Celery	Pepper Pot
Chicken	Printanier
Chicken-Gumbo	Tomato
Clam Chowder	Tomato-Okra
Consommé	Vegetable
Julienne	Vegetable-Beef
Mock Turtle	Vermicelli-Tomato

10 cents a can

LOOK FOR THE
RED-AND-WHITE LABEL

Campbell's Vegetable Soup

Campbell Kids
1940s

I N THE 1940s, WITH THE COUNTRY AGAIN AT WAR, THE CAMPBELL KIDS JOINED
their countrymen and diligently did their part. They served as war bond salesmen and air raid wardens, and, armed with bags proclaiming "Food Fights for Freedom," praised workers engaged in wartime production. Elsewhere, they planted victory gardens and beefed up soup recipes, too. "Here's a nourishing soup/For a nation at war," one Campbell Kid jauntily offered, "With more chicken in it/Than ever before!" It was clear their hard work was paying off. In 1944, the Kids were on hand to see the Campbell Soup Company receive an achievement award from the U.S. Department of War for its contributions to the nation's effort.

I dig and hoe
    With all my might.
The food I grow
    Will help the fight.

Who wants something new?
—and something awfully good!

IN CAMPBELL'S CREAM OF MUSHROOM WOMEN EVERYWHERE HAVE FOUND A NEW AND WELCOME FAMILY TREAT

You at your house will want to try Campbell's Cream of Mushroom Soup! Surely no one would willingly pass up such a delectable and unusual treat. Already, thousands of families are enjoying this soup often—thrilled with its rich creaminess, its deep mushroom flavor—delighted to find such an out-of-the-ordinary dish to brighten and vary their meals!

Campbell's are proud of their Cream of Mushroom Soup—proud as any home cook would be of a dish that turned out "just perfect." And *you* will be proud to serve it! Blended of extra-thick cream and plump young mushrooms—lavishly decked out with tender mushroom slices, it is indeed a rare and tempting dish! Steaming and savory, it makes people hungry the moment they see it; delicious and heart-warming, it makes them want to have it soon again.

So keep a supply of Campbell's Cream of Mushroom Soup always on hand—for regular family meals—for festive occasions—or to please an unexpected guest!

With tender young mushrooms,
To Campbell's I speed;
Those good cooks insist on
The finest, indeed!

Campbell's
CREAM of MUSHROOM

LOOK FOR THE RED-AND-WHITE LABEL

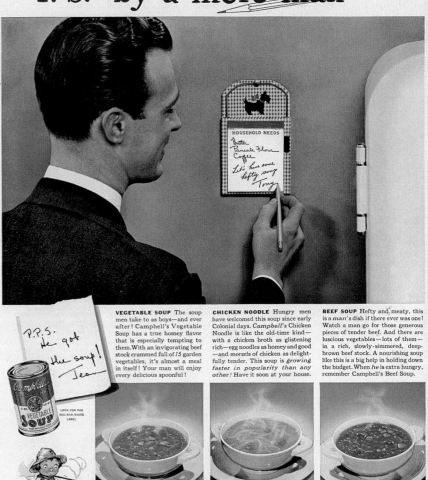

P.S.—by a mere man

HOUSEHOLD NEEDS

P.P.S. He got the soup! Jean

LOOK FOR THE RED-AND-WHITE LABEL

I'll send to Campbell's
For their use
The finest things
My fields produce!

VEGETABLE SOUP The soup men take to as boys—and ever after! Campbell's Vegetable Soup has a true homey flavor that is especially tempting to them. With an invigorating beef stock crammed full of *15* garden vegetables, it's almost a meal in itself! Your man will enjoy every delicious spoonful!

CHICKEN NOODLE Hungry men have welcomed this soup since early Colonial days. *Campbell's* Chicken Noodle is like the old-time kind—with a chicken broth as glistening rich—egg noodles as homey and good—and morsels of chicken as delightfully tender. This soup is *growing faster in popularity than any other!* Have it soon at your house.

BEEF SOUP Hefty and meaty, this is a *man's* dish if there ever was one! Watch a man go for those generous pieces of tender beef. And there are luscious vegetables—lots of them—in a rich, slowly-simmered, deep-brown beef stock. A nourishing soup like this is a big help in holding down the budget. When *he* is extra hungry, remember Campbell's Beef Soup.

Campbell's SOUPS

Clare, I've just discovered the most delicious new soup—Campbell's Cream of Mushroom! Joyce Bailey served it at her party yesterday.

Campbell's Cream of Mushroom? Why, that's already a favorite at our house. Jack says we can't have it too often for him!

THIS IS A SOUP that makes friends *quickly*! It's so delightful in taste that people want it often; so splendidly nourishing it fits well with family meals; so *unusual* that women call on it with confidence when special guests are coming . . . Smooth with the smoothness of extra-heavy cream, rich with the flavor of fresh young mushrooms and lavish with tender mushroom slices, Campbell's Cream of Mushroom is a treat indeed. When will coaxing plates of this tempting soup brighten eyes at *your* table?

Campbell's CREAM *of* MUSHROOM

I hear this conversation A dozen times a day: "Try Campbell's Cream of Mushroom, My dear, without delay!"

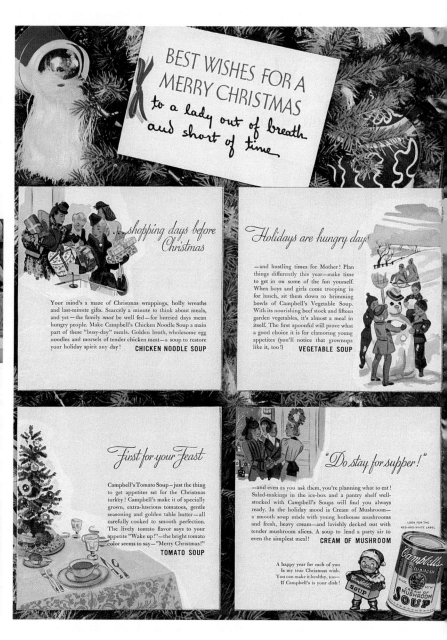

BEST WISHES FOR A MERRY CHRISTMAS to a lady out of breath and short of time

shopping days before Christmas

Your mind's a maze of Christmas wrappings, holly wreaths and last-minute gifts. Scarcely a minute to think about meals, and yet—the family *must* be well fed—for hurried days mean hungry people. Make Campbell's Chicken Noodle Soup a main part of these "busy-day" meals. Golden broth, wholesome egg noodles and morsels of tender chicken meat—a soup to restore your holiday spirit any day!

CHICKEN NOODLE SOUP

Holidays are hungry days

—and hustling times for Mother! Plan things differently this year—make time to get in on some of the fun yourself. When boys and girls come trooping in for lunch, sit them down to brimming bowls of Campbell's Vegetable Soup. With its nourishing beef stock and fifteen garden vegetables, it's almost a meal in itself. The first spoonful will prove what a good choice it is for clamoring young appetites (you'll notice that grownups like it, too!)

VEGETABLE SOUP

First for your Feast

Campbell's Tomato Soup—just the thing to get appetites set for the Christmas turkey! Campbell's make it of specially grown, extra-luscious tomatoes, gentle seasoning and golden table butter—all carefully cooked to smooth perfection. The lively tomato flavor says to your appetite "Wake up!"—the bright tomato color seems to say—"Merry Christmas!"

TOMATO SOUP

"Do stay for supper!"

—and even as you ask them, you're planning what to eat! Salad-makings in the ice-box and a pantry shelf well-stocked with Campbell's Soups will find you always ready. In the holiday mood is Cream of Mushroom—a smooth soup made with young hothouse mushrooms and fresh, heavy cream—and lavishly decked out with tender mushroom slices. A soup to lend a party air to even the simplest meal!

CREAM OF MUSHROOM

A happy year for each of you Is my true Christmas wish. You can make it healthy, too— If Campbell's is your dish!

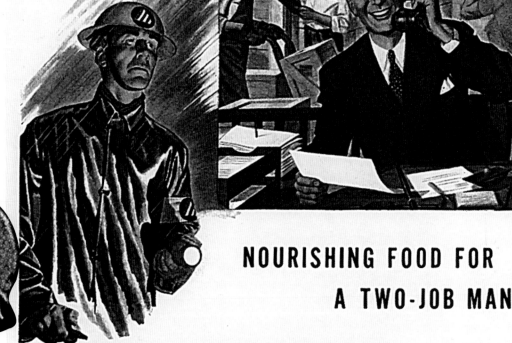

NOURISHING FOOD FOR
A TWO-JOB MAN

W HEN A DAY-JOB MAN takes on extra wartime duties he needs food he can work on, deserves food he can delight in. And good nourishing meals built around plates of hearty soup are just the thing for him. That is where Campbell's Soups come in.

Just tasting each of these hearty soups—tells you quickly that here is food that lifts a fellow's appetite and spirit. You get deep-down flavor . . . and nourishment to work and thrive on. When you build meals around these satisfying, homey soups, you have a lunch or supper to sustain and please a war-busy man.

Because of the needs of war, there is now less canned food for the home front. Sometimes you may not be able to get just the Campbell's Soup you'd planned on. If so, do try one of Campbell's other soups. Remember, each of them is food for times like these —food to keep war-busy people on their toes.

When working hard
Both day and night,
Good Campbell's Soup
Hits me just right.

Look for the
Red-and-White
Label

CHICKEN GUMBO SOUP

ALMOST A MEAL IN ITSELF
Here are fifteen tender vegetables steeped in a stock of fine beef—a soup rich with good things from the garden, hearty in flavor and filled with heartening nourishment for busy times like these.

Campbell's VEGETABLE SOUP

THICK, HE-MAN GOODNESS
A soup as Scotch as Highland heather—this old-fashioned combination of tender mutton, barley and vegetables is a mighty satisfying dish to set a man up for come what may.

Campbell's SCOTCH BROTH

BORROWED FROM OLD NEW ORLEANS
Here is a soup of the South adapted from an old Louisiana recipe. It's made of chicken, rice and okra and other fine garden vegetables, excitingly flavored with herbs and seasonings.

Campbell's CHICKEN GUMBO

Here's a nourishing soup
For a nation at war,
With more chicken in it
Than ever before!

Campbell Kids
1950s

THE WAR WAS OVER, THE G.I.s HAD RETURNED, AND THE 1950s BROUGHT
unprecedented prosperity, the spread of suburbia, and, of course, the Baby Boom.
Attention came back to domestic life, and so conditions were ripe for the Campbell
Kids' comeback. As television infiltrated American homes, the Kids got ready for their
first showbiz close-ups. Bearing a fresh modern look with spiffy new clothes, larger eyes,
and slightly squarer heads, they hit the big time on the small screen, singing "a song of
soup sense" and asking "Have you had your soup today?" on commercials for shows like
Lassie. By their official fiftieth birthday celebration in 1954, the Campbell Kids were
stars yet again. They were licensed on over sixty products that were made by thirty-four
companies and promoted in multi-page ads in *Life* magazine. Soon, children throughout
the country rode Campbell Kid bicycles, kept house with Campbell Kid vacuum cleaners,
wore Campbell Kid clothing, and even became proprietors of fiberboard Campbell Kid supermarkets
they could assemble at home.

from Columbus to Campbell

1544. In the first mention of the tomato in literature, Petrus Mattiolus says "this fruit, brought to Italy in our time, is eaten in the same manner as mushrooms—fried in oil with salt and pepper." Franco American Spaghetti came later.

1619. An "object of affection," the tomato was grown in France as an ornamental cover for garden houses and arbours. French settlers brought a new name, "*Pomme d'Amour*" or "Love Apple," and recipes for ketchup to New Orleans in the late 1700s.

1820. Many thought tomatoes poisonous. Robert Gibbon Johnson made himself famous by eating a whole basket of them on the courthouse steps of Salem, N. J. Many in the crowd went home to sample—cautiously—a love apple.

1839. People were growing tomatoes, but still growing the old primitive kinds. This year, for the first time, a prize was offered for the best tomato by the Massachusetts Horticultural Society. If only the judges could have seen the Campbell Tomato of 1955!

1865. First new American variety introduced. It originated as a chance seedling in a field in Iowa. Nowadays nature gets help from plant scientists at Campbell's four agricultural research laboratories in the United States and Canada.

1898. 406 years after Columbus, housewives discover a bright tasting new product in their stores—*Campbell's Tomato Soup*. Campbell set out to become tomato specialists. The tomato as we know it today still did not exist—but it was on its way.

1955.

The Campbell Tomato

It's the tomato flavor America knows best—the bright red juice, the glowing soup, the ketchup on the hamburger. It's the sauce on the spaghetti and the beans. Campbell's plant scientists and growers have never stopped trying to make it better, in line with our creed: "*To make the best, begin with the best . . . then cook with extra care.*"

"*We blend the best with careful pains
In skillful combination,
And every single can contains
Our business reputation.*"

Campbell's

Tomato Soup · Tomato Juice · Tomato Ketchup · Pork and Beans with Tomato Sauce
V-8 Cocktail Vegetable Juices · Franco-American Spaghetti (Tomato Sauce with Cheese)

All Aboard! Come join the fun!

Campbell Kids

Birthday Celebration

The Campbell Kids invite you to
their birthday celebration.
So turn the page, they've set the stage
in stores across the nation. ⟶

WALT DISNEY and MICKEY MOUSE ROUND UP THE KIDS for
MICKEY MOUSE CLUB
COPYRIGHT WALT DISNEY PRODUCTIONS
Campbell's
MICKEY MOUSE CLUB
C
ABC-TV
(83 stations)
EVERY
THURSDAY
5:15–5:30 pm
5:45–6:00 pm
Walt Disney's magic keeps Mickey Mouse Club (and lots of their parents) coming back for more, week after week.
Rex Allen, young film and TV star, tells kids the Campbell story, in the kind of talk they understand.
FOR CAMPBELL'S SOUPS, CAMPBELL'S PORK & BEANS, FRANCO-AMERICAN SPAGHETTI PRODUCTS

Soup and a sandwich—  that's for summer!

It's a combination as American as fireworks and the Fourth of July. A hot dog, hamburger or a ham-and-cheese. And soup. Campbell's Chicken Noodle Soup—the kind of soup that coaxes the appetite even on a wilting day.

Here's a soup everybody likes. There's the nourishment of chicken broth, simmered long and slowly to sparkling, golden goodness. Campbell's exclusive egg noodles, too —the most delicious noodles you ever had. And white and dark chicken meat, cubed generously—so tender you scarcely have to chew it!

How about cooking up some fun? For supper tonight, or the children's lunch tomorrow. Have soup and sandwiches— maybe Campbell's Chicken Noodle Soup!

Some day soon, do yourself a favor. Try our noodle soup for breakfast!

Once a day—
__every__ day—
SOUP!

M'm! M'm! Good!

Relaxing pause in a busy day . . . tempting bits of chicken in a golden chicken broth, smoothed to a creamy richness with sweet dairy cream.

So quick—so nutritious—so __simply__ delicious!

Campbell's Cream of Chicken Soup

Soup's on—
Enjoy it
any time!

The Campbell Kids SHOPPING GAME

Parker Brothers Inc.

AGES 5 TO 10

clip-
and
save!

Just keep these *Campbell Kids* in sight...

complete set
ONLY $1.00

Campbell Kids MIRRO BAKE SET

Everything tiny chefs need to bake and serve tasty treats. These beautifully-finished aluminum sets are safe, sanitary and rust-proof. 12-pc. Bake Set (shown above) includes Mixing Bowl, Tube Cake Pan, Biscuit Pan, Muffin Pan, Cooky Sheet, Tray, Scoop, Egg Whip, Dog, Rabbit, Chicken and Cat Cooky Cutters that really work!

Another favorite: *Campbell Kids Mirro 18-Pc. Coffee Set.* Includes Coffee Pot, Sugar Spoon, Butter Knife and 2 each, Plates, Cups, Saucers, Knives, Forks, Spoons, Napkins, beautifully packaged. *$1.00 set.*

ALUMINUM GOODS MFG. CO.
Manitowoc, Wisconsin

Whee!

Campbell Kids ROLLER SKATES

Winchester "tot-tailored" Skates have the Campbell Kids themselves right on the bright red package. These gleaming nickel and red beauties are made the sturdy, quality Winchester way... and are especially designed to fit the feet of your 5 to 8 year olds. Your youngsters will get years of body-building fun from these genuine junior

Skates. See them at your local dealer today...or send for *free* Winchester How-To-Skate booklet. Campbell Kids Roller Skates #3537...$2.95.
For free booklet, write to: Winchester Roller Skates Dept., Olin Mathieson Chemical Corp., New Haven 4, Conn.

WINCHESTER TRADE MARK

Famous *Campbell Kids* Sets for Meal-Time Fun!

Campbell Kids CHUCK WAGON SET

Every young frontiersman will love fixing real Western chow with this deluxe 20-piece cook set! Packed in a colorful Chuck Wagon Cabinet are two cans of Campbell's Soups...one can of Campbell's Pork and Beans...one can of Franco-American Spaghetti.

For fun there are two colorful fron-

tier neckerchiefs...a real phonograph record of popular Western tunes... Chuck Wagon Cook Book with real Western recipes. Rugged utensils include: real "Chow Kettle", two "Range Mugs", two "Chow Plates", two Forks, two Spoons, one Soup Ladle and one Stirring Spoon. $4.98*

Campbell Kids COOKING SET

Does she (or he) have a yen to be a real chef? There's a whole kitchen full of fun with this 20-piece set, filled with real cans of savory Campbell's Soups. There are six cans—four popular varieties. A gay "Pantry Shelf" Cabinet holds a genuine Wearever Aluminum Sauce Pan, Soup Ladle, Stirring Spoon,

two Princess Place Mats, Napkins, two Soup Bowls, two Soup Spoons, Pot Holder, two Crouton Cutters, and Measuring Cup.

The famous Campbell Kids are represented with a Chef's Apron and Hat ...and even a Campbell Kids Cook Book, full of tempting recipes. $4.98

Mfg. by **AMERICAN METAL SPECIALTIES CORP.**, Hatboro, Pa.

*PRICES SLIGHTLY HIGHER IN SOUTH AND WEST

with finer things...and better buys!

Campbell Kids SPORTSWEAR

Adorably flattering...these wonderfully designed outfits keep tiny misses looking their adorable best!

Shown above are a two-piece bolero suit made in both taffeta and felt and a fine cotton blouse sporting a Campbell Kids embroidered pocket.

The other model is wearing a Campbell Kids Jumper and a cotton blouse with an allover print of the Campbell Kids.

Also available, but not shown, are Campbell Kids Shirts and Slacks in sizes 2 to 12. See these reasonably priced youngsters' "separates" at your favorite children's department.

JUDY KENT SPORTSWEAR, Inc.
1370 Broadway, New York, N. Y.

Campbell Kids CHILDREN'S DRESSES

Two flattering models sure to make any tiny miss feel pampered. All tots love these gay well-designed dresses colorfully printed or embroidered with the lovable Campbell Kids. And mothers especially love the easy-to-wash, easy-to-press, spot-resistant qualities found in their fine "Good Behavior" broadcloth by Lowenstein. The pert allover print dress comes in aqua and pink. The embroidered model can be had in pink, caribbean blue, orchid. Both styles are exquisitely detailed...and are available at better stores everywhere. Sizes 1 to 3 at $4.98, and sizes 3 to 6x at $5.98.

TINY TOWN TOGS, INC.
1350 Broadway, New York 18, N. Y.

Campbell Kids POT 'N PAN HOLDER SET

Gay assets in any kitchen that no housewife should be without. Excellent protection against accidental burns and escaping steam. Set includes 2 Pot Holders, 2 slip-on Handle Holders, and 1 Oven Mitt. All are made of heavily quilted, durable, washable percale in attractive kitchen colors. The allover design shows the Campbell Kids making like merry chefs. Fine quality workmanship and washable fast colors make this set an exceptionally good value. Available individually or in sets in red, blue, green and yellow at stores everywhere. Complete 5-pc. set only $1.

EDLEN HERMAN PRODUCTS, INC.
4353 Orchard Street, Philadelphia 24, Penna.

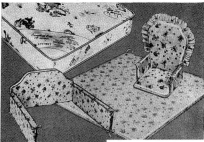

Campbell Kids KANTWE

Kantwet's fine quality, long-wearing nursery items in colorful, eye-appealing Campbell Kids designs. Shown above are the Crib Mattress...Play Pen Pad ...High Chair Pad...and the Hollywood Bumper Set for cribs. The entire set ...or each individual item...makes a wonderfully welcome, useful, and appreciated gift. Other Kantwet Nursery

Perfect for Summer- Soup 'n Sandwiches

Campbell Kids
1960s

THE 1960s WAS A TUMULTUOUS DECADE FOR THE UNITED STATES AS IT BECAME immersed in social change. Meanwhile, beginning in 1962, Campbell soup cans were thrust into the realm of Pop Art legend with the help of Andy Warhol. But as the Cold War got chillier, the U.S. entered Vietnam, and the Beatles invaded America, the Campbell Kids sat out on the sit-ins, stayed out of the fray, and largely kept out of the picture. However, as symbols of stability and an innocence on the wane, they were brought out to introduce the Campbell Soup Company's new Bounty Line and Red Kettle soups, and stayed on in company stockholder reports, on Christmas cards, and in the occasional television commercial. And, in at least one late-sixties ad, they were caught wearing paisley and putting flowers in their hair in an offer for a Campbell Kid poster that was described as "souper-delic!"

Sets them up for
school or play...
Soup 'n sandwich
every day!

INTRODUCING
THE CAMPBELL HANG-UP

A wild, wacky way to have your soup and get a way-out poster, too!

Turn your wall souper-delic! This poster's a "biggy" — 2 feet by 3 feet. Get it by sending in 3 different labels from either Campbell's Tomato, Vegetable Beef, Chicken, Vegetable, Chicken Gumbo, Chili Beef or Beef Noodle Soup and 50¢ with the coupon below. The Campbell Hang-Up. It'll make Campbell Kids everywhere say . . . M'm! M'm! Groovy!

To: Poster Offer, Box 411, Maple Plain, Minn. 55359

Name _____

Address _____

City _____ State _____ Zip _____

Offer expires Feb. 28, 1969. Good only in the U.S.A. and Puerto Rico. Subject to state and local regulations. Void if taxed, restricted or forbidden by law.

"To make the best, begin with the best—then cook with extra care."

This ad appeared 39 years ago...

"3-minute" men

About three minutes' preparation, and the biggest part of your meal is ready to eat—the best part too. Quickly prepared, delightful, wholesome, this splendid food is a favorite in the modern household.

Campbell's Tomato Soup

A purée of luscious red-ripe tomatoes fresh from the vines, daintily prepared in Campbell's famous kitchens, with choice creamery butter, granulated sugar and other savory ingredients. There are many tempting ways to serve it. Order a good supply and keep it handy.

12 cents a can

Have you checked the price of Campbell's Tomato Soup lately?

Anyone that goes to the store or pays the bills knows what's happened to prices over the years. That's why we thought you might be interested in this advertisement that ran for Campbell's Tomato Soup on July 2, 1921.

It shows that the price was 12¢ a can. If you have a grocery store advertisement handy —or if your memory is really good, we think you'll be mildly amazed to find that this is just about the same price you pay today . . . same size can, of course.

The same kind of price story—though in varying degree—can be told about the other Campbell's Soups.

Of course, we can't take all the credit. The happy reason that Campbell's has been able to buck the tide of rising prices is partly you, partly the grocer and farmer, and partly us. You, because there are so many more of you these days, and because you seem to like our soups more and more as time goes on. And it's the grocer and farmer, of course, because each has become increasingly efficient . . . the farmer in producing, and the grocer in serving you.

As for us, we just naturally like to make soup. We like to make it as good as we can and bring it to you for as little as we can. And we find ways to do this better as we go along.

This seems like a good time to tell you that we find this a very pleasant relationship, indeed—and we thank you.

Campbell's
Quality

Soups
Frozen Soups
Tomato Juice
Pork & Beans
• V-8 Cocktail Vegetable Juices
• FRANCO-AMERICAN Products
• SWANSON Products

Oyster Stew

There are only 3 ways to get it at its best

1. Move your kitchen to the seashore and make it yourself
2. Order it in a fine seafood restaurant
3. Buy Campbell's <u>Frozen</u>

One of the blessings of living near the seashore is having ocean-fresh oyster stew as often as you like (which for lots of people is pretty often).

But now, thanks to Campbell's freezing, your family can enjoy this same fine flavor *wherever* you live.

Campbell's makes it like the finest Boston oyster houses do. We cook plump young oysters in a hearty broth of milk, butter and special seasonings. Then we freeze it fast because that's the only way to keep the flavor as fresh as the moment we shucked the oysters.

When you can get oyster stew this good wherever you live, why don't you? Campbell's Frozen Oyster Stew. Fine eating, and fine nourishment, too—with an excellent balance of vitamins, proteins, and minerals.

Get it in your grocer's frozen food cabinet

Campbell's CONDENSED
FROZEN
FROZEN
OYSTER STEW SOUP

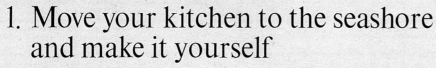

Old-Fashioned Vegetable with Beef • Cream of Potato • Cream of Shrimp
Clam Chowder (New England Style) • Green Pea with Ham • Oyster Stew

F ROM ACTIVISM AND DISCO TO OIL SHORTAGES AND WATERGATE, THE 1970s

were not quiet times, though the Campbell Kids remained low-key. But, while they had yet to regain a strong advertising presence, they were still anything but forgotten. In 1971, artist Richard Edmiston began a twenty-year tenure that would see the Kids evolve like never before. Meanwhile, the 1970s also saw them make sporadic comebacks—on mugs, in memorabilia, and as dolls in countries from Mexico to Japan—that would prove their cosmopolitan appeal. And while that decade's afros, bell bottoms, and leisure suits weren't quite the Kids' style, they were back in their element as they commemorated the nation's bicentennial in full colonial garb.

A loving cup from Campbell's
(For just 2 Noodle-O's labels and 60¢)

We'll name a bowl after
(For 75¢ and 2 labels from Campbell's Alphab

M'm! M'm!
Good!

Get a ceramic Campbell Kid Bo
tom. Just send your name plus
or Vegetarian Vegetable So
with somebody's name in e
Plain, Minnesota 55359,
1971. Void if taxed, restric
four weeks for delivery.

The name I want in the b
One name only! Limit: 9

NAME
ADDRESS
CITY STAT

Send in now for your two-fisted mug.
Get one of these colorful thermal mugs for every little Campbell Kid
in your family! It keeps hot soup hot, milk and juices cold. Best of all,
it makes eating fun! For each mug, just send 2 labels from any
Campbell's Noodle-O's Soups and 60¢ to: **Two-Fisted Mug, Box 652,
Maple Plain, Minnesota 55359.**

Your Name
(please print)

Address

Noodle-O's are the
neat-eating soups from
Campbell's. Chicken
Noodle-O's, Golden
Vegetable Noodle-O's, and
Tomato-Beef Noodle-O's.
All three made with oodles
of unspillable noodles

budget.

meals all you splurge on is flavor.

HI...

5. Beef Noodle Soup ▪ **Hero sandwich** ▪ **Butterscotch pudding** ▪ A supper that's light... just right for a Sunday night.

6. Chicken Gumbo Soup ▪ **Luncheon meat sandwich** ▪ **Pie and milk** ▪ An all-American lunch for any day of the week.

7. Chicken Vegetable Soup ▪ **Frankfurter** ▪ **Ice cream and milk** ▪ An indoor picnic that's a great supper any time.

Campbell's in the cupboard is like money in the bank.

HAPPY BIRTHDAY

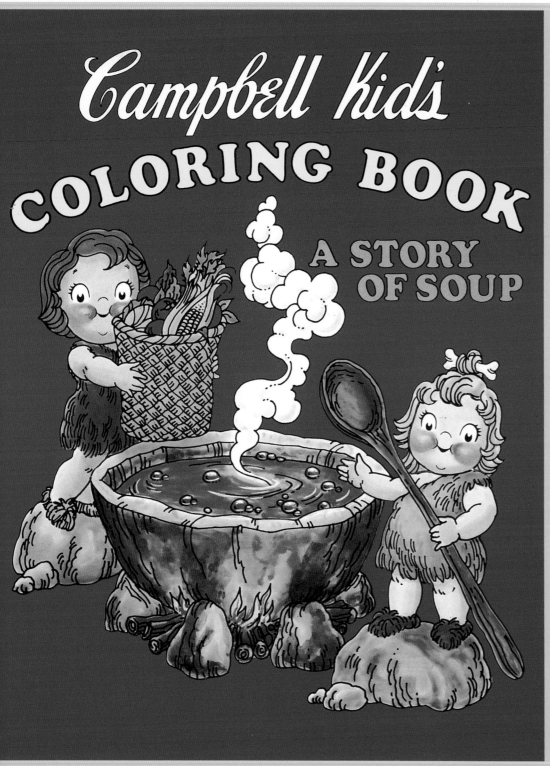

THE CAMPBELL KIDS BEGAN THE 1980s WITH CAPTAIN AMERICA, URGING
energy conservation amid lingering oil worries and looming recession. But the decade soon turned into the go-go years and the Kids were again on the move. Early on, the Campbell Kid Collection brought vintage Kid images to everything from sleeping bags and serving trays to watches and neckties. But not content to be relegated to history, the Kids soon powered up in new power suits for a 1987 *Business Week* cover that pronounced them "Marketing's New Look." Despite their yuppie transformation, however, the Kids had hardly sold out to the Me Generation. They snapped into action for causes like improving youth fitness by slimming down and getting into shape themselves. They took up soccer, basketball, gymnastics, and weightlifting, and then added skiing and ice skating with the Campbell Soup Company's involvement in the 1984 Sarajevo Winter Olympics and, in subsequent years, U.S. figure skating as well. Meanwhile, they diversified to reflect America's changing complexion, appeared in brochures promoting healthy self-esteem, and even boarded a blimp floating high above the Farm Aid concert that raised money for rural families. They were once again helping Americans mark time, and so it was only natural that they began appearing every year in their very own calendars, too.

Whoever
you are...

YOU'RE
'SOUPER'
THE WAY YOU ARE!

When competition is healthy fun
then victory is dearer
For knowing with each mighty serve
the Campbell's Soup is nearer!

Campbell's
"HARVEST OF GOOD FOODS"
∽❦∽ Fall 1987 ∽❦∽

W HILE THE 1990s BEGAN WITH A RECESSION-INDUCED WHIMPER, THE
Campbell Kids were as energetic as could be. Their workout regimens were by now a healthy habit, as they perservered in sports like hockey and soccer, and unflaggingly kept the weight off. Trekking on mountaintops and even paragliding, they were now living the '90s active lifestyle, testing their physical limits while pushing their minds as well. They worked at the computer, and studied hard in school, and reveled in their multiculturalism in an age of globalization.

But they were still kids at heart, and, as kids, they had fun while they listened to boom boxes, kickflipped their skateboards, and continued to relive history on idyllic countryside excursions, and in early-twentieth-century dress. Indeed, they were looking both forward and back, and found crafty new expression in traditional paper dioramas as well as digital animation.

Our parachutes fill
in a warm blustery breeze;
with the Power of Campbell's,
we sky dive with ease.

NEVER
UNDERESTIMATE
THE POWER OF
Campbell's™

HAVING SURVIVED THE Y2K SCARE, THE KIDS ARE STARTING THE TWENTY-
first century by proving their versatility in more and more surprising ways. New technology has not only brought them to
their keyboards, but has also drawn them in the round with the first digi-
tally rendered, 3-D Campbell Kids making their entrance in advertisements and calendars. Meanwhile, they've joined the craze for all things
retro, dressing up once again as flappers, '30s radio stars, and even World
War II heroes to show they haven't forgotten their past.

Campbell Kids
...AND TOMORROW

WHILE THE CAMPBELL SOUP COMPANY IS CELEBRATING THE KIDS' PAST one hundred years, it's also looking toward their future. DePersico Creative Group has dreamed up different ways to keep the Kids as relevant and fresh as ever. Artists Jeff Marshall, Joe Masterson, Maureen Keenan, Michael Adams, and Connie Beecher have illustrated a host of possibilities. These ideas include separating the Campbell Kids into three peer groups to appeal to a broader age range, from toddlers to preteens. Members of these new coteries would take on the personalities of everyone from the artsy bohemian and the techno-geek to the fashionista, skater, hip-hopper, rollerblader, and high school jock. Other ideas call for rendering the Kids in a range of styles, such as *anime,* to reflect contemporary aesthetics.

No matter the final result of these explorations, one thing remains certain: As they embark on their second century, the Campbell Kids will remain true to the virtues and qualities for which they are known and will continue to delight generations of Americans.

Campbell Kids

ACKNOWLEDGMENTS

My sincere thanks go to the Campbell Soup Company, and especially David Oates, who lent his enthusiastic support and helpful guidance throughout this project. Tremendous gratitude goes to Campbell archivist Beth Bartle, without whose patience, assistance, and insight this book would not have been possible. In addition, I'd like to thank John Fleckner and Kay Peterson of the Smithsonian Institution, as well as the many Campbell Kid collectors who so eagerly offered their help. Special thanks to editor Linas Alsenas and designers Elizabeth Morrow-McKenzie and Vivian Cheng for their help in bringing everything together.   —A.C.